Lo[.]
Be

Volume 1

"Love *Be*" is an illustrated collection of heartfelt poetry and prose on the topics of Unconditional Love, Peace and the pathway of Awakening.

Compassionately finding beauty in the natural world, ourselves and each other — empowering meditative exploration of our human experience and the profound nature of reality.

This book of original, exclusively human-written poetry, emphasises the power of conscious intent and inspires ways to find, and to be, the unconditional love that many hope to see and experience in this often challenging world.

Bonus chapter: "Wishes" - poetic Irish Blessings for your happiness and well-being.

Written and illustrated by,
Michèle L. Carbery

"Love *Be*"

Writing, illustration and book design

by Michèle L. Carbery

COPYRIGHT © 2025 Michèle L. Carbery

All rights reserved under International, British, European and Pan-American Copyright Conventions.

By payment of the required fees, you have been granted the non-exclusive, non-transferable right to access and read the text of this book. No part of this text or the illustrations may be reproduced, transmitted, downloaded, or stored in or introduced into any information storage and retrieval system, in any form or by any means, whether electronic or mechanical, now known or hereinafter invented, without the express written permission of the author.

First Edition

Version 1

ISBN: 9798282581119

Imprint: Independently published

"Unconditional Love is the compass."

To Jan,

With fond memories of your kindness, creativity, generosity, lovely smile and warm & welcoming friendship. Your friendship made a big difference in my life 2012 – 2014 (hard to believe this is now well over a decade ago!) and I have never forgotten. ♡

I hope you and your lovely family are very well.

With love,
Michèle   AUG 29, 2025.

Contents

Love Be

The Only Thing 3
The Invitation 5
Between the Heavy Stones. 7
Unconditional Love 9
Guiding Moon 11
Silver Birch Leaf 13
Smile Be-ing 1 15
Thought Sands 17
Beyond the Froth 19
Vapourware Anchors 21
Looking 23
Love Be. 25
Quantum Computing 27
Edgeless 29
What is Love 31
Earth and Sky Connector 33
Rain on the Pond. 35
Transforming Impermanence 1. 37
Stories on the Cinema Screen 39
Interlude: The Wind and the Twig. 41
Fog in the Breeze and Sunlight 43
Solubeauty. 45

The Chance	47
Cloud Teachings 1	49
Turning the Keys to a Great Day	51
Freedom from Drama	53
Silent Pool	55
Love is... Something More	57
Love is... Listening	59
Sea-ing	61
Special Shoes	63
Balanced	65
Living Prayer	67
Fireflies	69
The Lunch Meeting	71
Food of Life	73
Between Now and Now	75
Divergence	76
Perspective	79
The Space Between the Seconds	83
Tree Gazing 1	85
Interlude: Murmeration	87
Invisible Owl	89
Hidden in the Woods	91
Magic-making	93
A Million, Million Mossy Minds	95
Leaf	97
Shallow Puddle	99
Cloud Teachings 2	103
Losing, Not Losing	105

Three Things 107
Things to potentially unlearn 109
This Day, for "Sun" 111
Causes..................................... 113
Interlude: Skylark Moment 115
Kaleidoscope Dreams........................ 117
Record Player 119
Peace-fuel................................. 121
Shape-shifting............................. 123
The Wind 125
The Steadied Particle 127
Birdsong, Soul Song 129
Light Presence............................. 131

Wishes

A wish for the journey of you............... 135
A wish for your spring-times 137
A wish for your present moment.............. 139
A wish for your wellness.................... 141
A wish for your community 143
A wish for your beautiful light............. 145

MEDITATION 149
KIND WORDS FOR A TROUBLED WORLD.... 151
ABOUT THIS BOOK 153
THANK YOU 155
DEDICATION 157

Chapter 1

Love Be

Love *Be*

The Only Thing

The only thing
that really matters

in every
moment

is

whether, or not,
there is

Love

in our mind
and heart.

Love *Be*

The Invitation

A dream within a dream.
The invitation to awaken
and be fully present.

Consciously alive
with exquisite awareness.
Yet, passionately peaceful.

Sensing Love beneath
surface perceptions.
Striving to live harmlessly.

Seeing the boundless beauty
we had forgotten
within the illusion of surfaces.

Reconnecting with
immeasurable kindness.
Creating, the next moment.

Becoming the Love.
Becoming the invitation.

Kindness Grows

Between the Heavy Stones

Delicately, between the heavy stones
that those who have weighty voices call real,

exists a web of Love and life,
like the subtle mushroom matrix of tree speech.

Wisdom, hidden within the fragile
filteranium of quiet, subtle pathways.

Alive with bifurcating touch;
sharing, exchanging and creating.

Living within the changing spaces
between the heavy stones,

forming a precious supporting web
of Love and kindness.

Holding the entire world,
together.

Love *Be*

Unconditional Love

Born from respect, compassion,
a wish to give,
to nurture,
to relieve suffering,
to see others

happy.

Love, with no transactions
nor expectations.

Love that surpasses
everything ordinary,

the blissful kindness
given to ourself and others.

Love *Be*

Guiding Moon

The primal peace of
moonlight shining
through Winter
twigs of a Great Oak
a Poplar and a Yew.

We gaze into the glowing
silence, using the vision
sense of ourselves
our pre-selves and ancestors,
all present, now.

Frosty grass gently
crackles as we step forward
into the relentless uncertainly
of what may lay ahead,
trusting that guiding light

travelling with us
like the moon.

The precious peaceful,
loving Guide appearing
when we need them.
Around and inseparably within,
when our heart is listening.

Love *Be*

Silver Birch Leaf

Silver birch leaf
tethered, yet free,
moving as the sky breathes.

Owning,
then releasing the
sun's freely-given body.

Gentle flickering,
like green
butterfly wings,

floating in the sky
upon the graceful
breathing tree.

Leaf has never been
in the same place
in space and time.

We are like this, too
even in the appearance
of standing still.

Listening,
while Nature whispers
'Peace'.

Smile Be-ing 1

We smiled with Love,
gently from our hearts,
and felt the world
smile with us.

We smiled,
and a sun
fell into the
heart of a stone

and crystals
hidden within
glittered, glowed and
flowed to the surface.

We smiled
and a tear
turned into
a rainbow.

Love *Be*

Thought Sands

We find pathways
in old and new places.

Paths created and walked
for a very long time.

Thought sands of years,
ancestral inner chantings.

Sands flowing over rock
wear deepening tracks.

Some pathways lead to
beautiful places.

Some pathways lead to
thorns and precipices.

Pathways inside
are reflected outside.

Love *Be*

Beyond the Froth

This bubbled up to a surface
that has no surface.
Appearing as the fizzing froth
of material and mind existence.

A froth that dissolves into no 'thing'
and is made of no 'thing'

yet functions.

So we flowered senses with which to
experience this rolling moment
in no-time, no-place,
filled with all potentials.

We gave these perceptions names –
creating here and there, self and other.

Localised perceptions could become an 'i'.

Now, may we strive to see
beyond the screen
pervasively painted by our mind
and by the causes we create(d).

Learning to function as living Love,
for that was surely the original intention.

Love *Be*

Vapourware Anchors

How quickly the things we thought we wanted,
may become chains.

Vapourware anchors in time and space,
made of that which appears to provide happinesss.

Yet, nothing can remain stable or secure.
Change releases and recycles.

We weigh ourselves down creating anchors,
dreaming of keeping that which can never be kept.

Mindful observation reveals our anchors,
creating opportunity for choice.

Releasing anchors need not be external,
Inner wisdom and Love are the keys.

Love *Be*

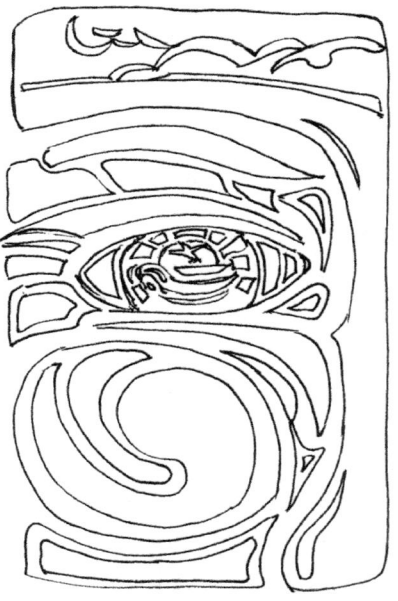

Looking

Looking into the eyes of a beloved being
seeing the universe, ourself,
everything and no-thing,
reflected.

Looking into the eyes of a beloved being
realising we are seeing
our own
mind.

Tenderly holding a beloved being,
feeling their energy and our own.
The edges of our forms
dissolving

into the blissful emptiness
of everything.
All things.
One.

Love *Be*

Love *Be*

Gently through life,

quietly,

invisibly,

choose,

to Love

Be.

Love *Be*

Quantum Computing

One day soon,
we will know
we no longer need to wait,
because the questions we ask
will already have been answered
before we asked them.

And, the things
we wished for
will already have been created,
or have happened,
before we realised
we had wished for them.

What we did not know
is that we did not need
to build a computer.
The mechanism already existed
within and around each of us.

We have been using it every day,
wisely, or unwisely,
to create our own reality.

Love *Be*

Edgeless

Love, beyond the sense of
limited ' i '.

Love, showing us

that the appearance of finite edges to
people and things

is illusory.

Love, dissolving the concept of
self and other,
opening the door to
a quiet contented heart.

Opening the door to
unencumbered

inner peace and joy.

Love *Be*

What is Love

Beyond fear.
Beyond conditions.
Beyond expectations.
Beyond form and beyond thought.
Beyond self and other.

Beyond,
yet, here, right now.
Limitless expansion.
Acute formless connection
in the purest way possible.

Powerful.
Profound, beyond measure.
A Peace. An unsurpassed
flow of Love and Peace
that is our true home.

Love *Be*

Earth and Sky Connector

Gazing through misted glass at a tree.
Its graceful height reaching out of sight
beyond the window frame.

The seam where Tree emerges from the ground
is heaved and lifted from decades of
gentle striving.

The vertical stem a gracefully-growing spire
connecting to the sky.
Vibrant, assured, free and gift-giving.

As if the Earth itself is reaching for the sky,
Reaching for the sun, reaching to touch
water-kissed air.

Tree's gentle, determined mission supports life,
This earth and sky connector
harmonizes and nurtures.

When we gently touch Tree with mind and hand,
we gently touch all
Earth, water, air, light and life.

Love *Be*

Rain on the Pond

The water surface opens
in response to the impact
and recloses, launching
a droplet above the surface.
It hovers while forces equalize,
then falls back into the oneness.

It is raining over the pond.

The water in the droplets
and the pool into which they fall
has been in the steamy breath of
dinosaurs and waterfalls,
the tears of mothers
and the blood of

every living being that ever lived.

Immeasurable drops and ripples,
since beginningless time,
intersecting,
interacting,
within the perceptions of
minds creating the appearance

of this rolling moment, now.

Love *Be*

Transforming Impermanence 1

May this Love-filled day
shine with calm clarity
about the nature of reality.
This functioning rolling moment,
empty of anything permanent.

May all pain of impermanence
become a wisdom sense
about external appearance.
Transforming, without pause,
into loving compassion for all.

May Love and Peace increase,
seeing each moment cease,
potentials arise in consciousness.
Causes and conditions roiling,
like bubbles in a fizzing ocean.

May loving responsibility
steer the ship through the sea,
giving kindness unceasingly.
Tears of light will dry the ocean.
All transformed through compassion.

Love *Be*

Stories on the Cinema Screen

The Light was dimmed
by layers of compounded illusions,
solidified through countless eons
into a shell of scratched and frosted glass
upon which plays our own cinematic movie.

Many teachers have spoken of this,
presenting their profound messages
upon the noisy screens
of all who could, and would, listen.
Joyfully, illuminating, they said,

"Be brave enough to choose Love,
to clean clouds from the mind screen.
One day, the hazy screen will soundlessly dissolve,
revealing a pure Light of Love,
releasing us into everything we can be."

Love *Be*

Interlude:
The Wind and the Twig

The wind, water and Tree offered me a twig.

It slowly floated to the shore upon diagonal ripples. I cherished this twig and put it in a glass of water.

And so, an intersection appeared – the continuum of the tree and my own – within a moment. Within a world, of intangible 'moments'.

Together, with the light of the Sun and the water of clouds that have traversed the skies of Earth before life awakened, the twig grew roots and fresh life emerged.

I tenderly planted Tree's new self in a new place and the continuum of Tree expanded.

Yet, Tree does not forget who she is, for the causes and conditions that created her continue to flow.

If Tree has a sense of "I am" where will she feel the edges of her Self to be now?

Perhaps inseparably within everything, and no thing.

We can feel like this, too.

Love *Be*

Fog in the Breeze and Sunlight

In the middle of the night
dream experiences appear
with great clarity and reality.
Yet, by morning they disappear,
like fog in the breeze and sunlight.

Experiences of waking life are the same.
Each perception passing to the next.
Our thoughts and feelings, creating
nothing tangible that can be held for long,
like fog in the breeze and sunlight.

Knowing this
what are we to do with our time?
What are we to do with this appearance?
What are we to do with this changing moment?
The answer may be very simple,
choose Love.

Love *Be*

Solubeauty

A thought, 'nice sky today'
at seeing glimpses of pure treasure.

Radiant blue within rafters of grey cloud edges
at which no one is looking.

One world filled with awe, but others walk by
each carrying their consciousness in a hand-held box.

So a mind soars alone within the beauty
of the blue they do not see.

Experiencing beauty in isolation is its own feeling.

It needs a name, for everything is nothing
if it does not have a name.

Isojoy? Beaulone? Alonbliss? Solubeauty.

Solubeauty seems best shared with,
and dissolved into, unconditional Love.

Love *Be*

The Chance

Inner peace and happiness
lead to outer peace and happiness

for ourselves, each other
and for all precious beings

with whom we share
a solitary sphere of
rock, water and air.

Together on a spinning globe
in an edgeless dark vacuum.

This is our time.
The joy-filled chance
to get it right.

Love *Be*

Cloud Teachings 1

We are more like clouds
than we think.

Our thoughts and feelings
like mists, scudding across the clear sky.

The floating mists gather into cumulous
when we focus on them.

A focus upon Peace and Kindness
demists clouds into clear sky.

A focus on resentments, anxieties or blame
solidifies clouds into pain,

accreting mists into towering thunderheads,
raining and thrashing with lightning.

Only to later dissolve away
into a clear sky.

The peaceful mind sky is the firmament
upon which our heavy clouds appear.

The solidity of sky and clouds
unfindable.

Love *Be*

Turning the Keys to a Great Day

Looking for the
good qualities of others
instead of our own.

Looking for the
beauty in our world
instead of the disappointing.

Looking for the
Peace in our world
instead of the disturbing.

Looking for the
harmony in our life
instead of the disputes or difficulties.

Extending a hand of friendship
to a person or animal,
instead of not noticing them.

Looking for
daily opportunities to enjoy a
feeling of gratitude.

Love *Be*

Freedom from Drama

Unconditional Love is
calm and clear.
No drama here.

No pull or push.
No sticky attachment.
No resisting or controlling.

Feeling as light and free
to give,
as to receive.

Yet as deep as a fjord,
as big as an ocean
and endless like the wind.

Love *Be*

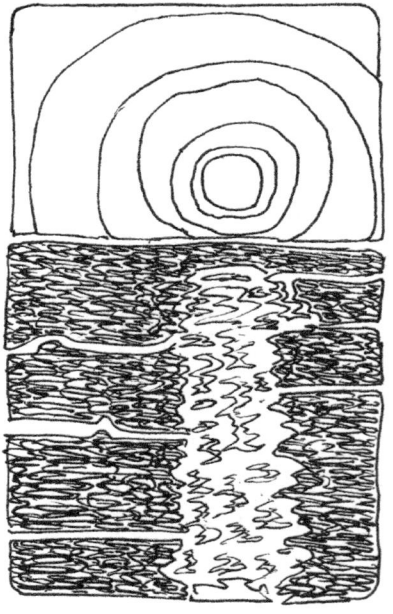

Silent Pool

In the quiet
of the night,
neither asleep,
nor awake.

In gentle,
weightless,
floating.

No self manifests.
Peaceful.
Safe.
No place.
No time.

Soundless calm.
Waves of indigo.
Rain of light,
as word droplets.

Insight splashes,
invisibly,
into a quietened,
silent pool
of mind.

Love *Be*

Love is... Something More

Aspiring to be
more than we thought we could be.

To all of those who have Loved unconditionally
for the benefit of others,

traversing their spiritual path with faith

who have dedicated themselves purely
to Peace and Compassion,

who have surpassed ordinary, meaningfully.

May we become just like you.

Love *Be*

Love is... Listening

Sometimes
Love
is simply

listening.

*Really
listening.*

Without expecting,
comparing,
advising,

or fixing.

*Just
listening.*

Love *Be*

Sea-ing

Flying white crosses scream gullabies.
Sand rises in just the
right places to massage our feet.

Wind brushes clear our skin and mind,
tickling our hair and
filling our breathing bodies.

Boundless sea gems so exquisite in colours
we can almost taste
the sparkling hues of blue and green.

Waves roar to us a loud Peace,
washing away busy thought.
we become pleasantly empty, yet filled

with peaceful Love.

Love *Be*

Special Shoes

If we were lucky,
we managed to step over the
eggshells and glass,
the distortions of others,
their ancestors and societies,

into our own shoes made of a
special material called
Loving Faith.

These special shoes carry both
the one who searched to
understand and heal,
and the stronger one
who found hope,

leading the way forward
with clarity, in calm, kind
self confidence.

On a journey to complete surpassing
of old concepts and illusions,
we are strong enough
to journey through life
as one, with a happy peace, because,

we chose Love.

Most days anyway.
We found a path that suits us well now,
in our peaceful freedom.

Love *Be*

Balanced

Unconditional Love balanced
with calm wisdom.

Compassionate clarity and wise actions
to protect and help ourselves, and others.

Yet, with a more peaceful mind
and a beneficial motivation within,

actions increase peace and happiness in the world
and in our hearts.

Love *Be*

Living Prayer

Love, as one heart,
quietly,
invisibly,

praying for the whole world.

Love *Be*

Fireflies

Fireflies along the path

in the samsaric gloom
within the shifting room
of collective mind.

Diamond flashes and steady glows,

lighting the way
like stepping stones
through the illusion.

Closer together the illuminations flow,

beyond 'here' and 'there'
the path dissolves
in a wisdom glow.

Love *Be*

The Lunch Meeting

After great enthusiasm,
the idea was softly poached
and placed between slices of
I'm not sure.

A lost dream of
what could have been,
Words of surface objectivity,
no meaning, spiritually.

Yet, profundity in
surface mundane-ocrity
comes from the mind
within. Heartfelt regard

respect and kindness
transforming
mistaken perceptions of
ordinary, into

supramundane appreciating.

Love *Be*

Food of Life

Love is like food,
water and light.

Without Love,
living beings fail to flourish.

Even one small, kind gesture
can mean the world

and will keep another's Light
shining bright.

Love *Be*

Between Now and Now

There are treasures
to be found
in the space
between

now and now.

If you look,
go gently.
Anchor yourself
on each side
of this moment
and feel safe

to investigate,

with peaceful Compassion
for yourself
and for all living beings.

It is OK. You are not alone.
We are all in this together.

Divergence

Consciousness,
walking the line,
formed of the indiscernible
no line, that is empty
at every point.

Walking the non-line,
between,
'I' and 'other',
'here' and 'there',
and what 'will be'.

Between,
'light' and 'dark',
'thing' and 'no-thing',
each created out of
divergence.

Infinite bifurcation.
Dual aspects,
dividing instantly
and endlessly
within perception.

So 'nothing'
can become,
'something' in name
and, function as such,
within our mind.

An inner question,
what is in the space
between this and that?
Or, between self and other?
Investigate softly.

Love *Be*

Perspective

Love, given from a lighter heart

shines generously

with a bigger perspective.

A much bigger perspective.

Love *Be*

We are TIME
    TRAVELLERS
in a world of
NON-TIME

Love *Be*

The Space Between the Seconds

Yes, find a
Quiet place.

Let no one and no thing
interrupt your
exploration of the
space between the seconds.

Inner Peace is your right.
Claim it in your heart,
own it in your days,
yet remain harmless

and kind
in your gentle
quickening
striving for it.

Love *Be*

Tree Gazing 1

The restful peace
in eyes, mind and heart
tree gazing with Love.

Tree was alive
long before I was
anything.

Silently growing
giving life
unconditionally.

Giving air to breathe
Giving homes to the birds
who grace our skies and ears.

The bold bifurcating
branches and twigs
etching the sky.

Manifested from sun and water,
asking for nothing more
than the space and grace

to be.

Love *Be*

Interlude: **Murmeration**

Orange and purple light glows in the soft underceiling of evening clouds.

A smoke-like shadow moves and swirls, low across the sky, momentarily reaching upwards from the horizon, expanding like mesh, then flowing back into moving emulations of solid forms.

Temporarily appearing as the flowing shapes of animals and birds, then transitioning suddenly into a noisy grey haze of scintillating dots – rippling wingbeat waves of wheeling starlings.

Within each starling's form, uncountable constellations of tiny stars are set within reflective dark feathers. Diamonds floating in a sheen of metallic purple and green.

Each bird flying freely, yet together, creating the appearance of a living organism. Existing in no singlular time, space or place.

A consciousness awake within each bird, wanting to be alive, wanting to have food, water and shelter. Wanting to be safe, protected, free from suffering and to be happy.

Watching, we live with them in that murmeration, as individuals and in the form of their collective being.

A quiet place in our heart, illuminated by Love and Nature's beauty, awakens us to our onenness.

Love *Be*

Invisible Owl

Tawny owl calls
from the velvety dark
guilded by shapes of soft indigo.

Faint twilight sky,
barely discernable
from the black silhouettes

floating as absences
on jasmine scented air
across glowing, rippling water.

Breath barely moving, waiting.

A faint rustle of delicate
bat wings, swerving,
diving, avoiding, catching.

While one life ends,
another exclaims,
and awareness meets

the owl's next call in midair.
The pensive tension,
gratefully broken.

Love *Be*

Hidden in the Woods

There is a place in
the Stillwater forest,
between cabin and quonset,
where the word
'Kindness'
may still live.
Written into wet concrete
by my younger hand.

Instead of a name
was written
a wish for
Kindness to flourish,
for all the natural
beings of the forest,
mountains, skies
and crystal waters.

All things change.
Snow, ice and shovels
will transform the concrete
path into dust and sand.
Yet, may the wish still live.
Grains of Kindness
carried on the soles of boots
and pathways of mind,

into the forest and the world.

Love *Be*

Magic-making

Making a day magical,
beauty-finding and seeing,
without seeking to own anything.

Choosing to see beauty,
a forgotten form of Love.
A form of Kindness.

A way of living and giving,
to oneself and others.
gratefully

and unconditionally.

Love *Be*

A Million, Million Mossy Minds

Mossy softness,
spawning green filaments.
A million, million of our ancestors,
in one small patch of scented earth.

Living alongside us,
now,
quietly
being.

Reproducing like mammals and fish,
yet with the pale blood of trees.
Colonies flowing to the rounded edge,
of the rippling river life engine.

Alive with light flowing through
countless, sparkling water droplets
in the form of mini worlds,
floating in a universe of green.

Within each fragile shining sphere,
held lightly on tiny green points
with the most delicate touch,
keeping the preciousness safe.

Honoring the worlds that are present now,
and, the worlds waiting to happen.

Love *Be*

Leaf

We are each like a
Leaf,
upon a tree of Loving Kindness and
the work of our ancestors.

Leaf starts life as a Spring bud
opening into a soft green form,
nurtured by the tree of life
upon which Leaf depends.

Leaf ages as Summer rises
becoming strong and darker green.
Energy flows back from Leaf
into the tree and outward into the air.

The surge of Summer sun eases into Autumn
and crinkles appear on Leaf's form.
Green fades to gold and red.
Leaf gives life now in gentle ways.

Finally, yet without ending, Leaf gives back
what has been given, then fades and falls.
Reaching the Earth, without sentiment, gracefully
yielding and transforming.

This is a journey that belongs to us all,
and will one day seem as just a moment.

So, may we be as kind and tender to those
who are presently experiencing Autumn,
as we are to those who are
presently experiencing Spring.

Shallow Puddle

Evaporating quickly
like a shallow puddle,
unhappy feelings disappear
in the breeze of peaceful thoughts.

Each lacking substance
beyond that which is given
by name, word and narrative.
Yet, not lacking meaning.

As the dark-edged mind cloud
disappears over the horizon,
our inner sun emerges
clearing the way to a blue sky day.

Our inner Peace and Love
is uncovered
and once again
free to shine.

Love *Be*

*Gently softening
the edges of our
mind-built sense
of self, opens doors to
sunlit inner pathways
through which new
levels of peace,
love, joy and
understanding
can flow.*

Love *Be*

Cloud Teachings 2

We are more like
clouds
than we think.

Above the fluffy
inner narrative
of names, words and pictures,

the sky is
calm, quiet, spacious,
observing.

Love *Be*

Losing, Not Losing

I knew it was coming.
For a long time, I knew.
Yet, still in disbelief and confusion,
it appeared as if her life spirit,
the essence of everything she was,
had dropped to the ground and
rolled away into
another world,

leaving only the biological machinery
that had carried her pure soul.

Whenever I find one of
her little hairs
around the house
reflexively I protect it,
tenderly pick it up and
place it in a small envelope.
Collecting them,
as if trying to rebuild her.

Twelve years of Love
mixed with attachment.

The part that is Love
is pain-free and forever.

Love *Be*

Three Things

Three things at a time.
When done, three more.
Choosing the positive
and beneficial, right now.

A way to move
through difficult times,
when complexity, pain and noise
seem to be all around.

Yet more is possible.
One of three with Gratitude.
One of three with Kindness.
Once of three with Love.

Until all three become one.
A loving joy and peace
manifests in the mind,
then one day, in everything we do.

Love *Be*

Things to Potentially Unlearn

How did society ever decide
that showing and sharing
natural, innocent
Kindness and Love
is 'weakness'?

Or, that
daydreaming
and gazing at Nature
in wonder and Peace
is a 'waste of time'?

It is potentially worth unlearning these 'lessons'.

Scribble colour joyfully.
Free your spirit
with child-like glee
embracing all the beauty,
peace and possibility.

Love *Be*

This Day, for "Sun"

Emerging from dreams, sleepily still awaking,
A glow of yellow sunshine transforms the curtain,
into luminous, curving, unmoving waves.

Bright beams of light racing beyond the fabric veil,
proclaiming the potentials of this moment,
calling me to wake-up, to move, to live.

The brightness increasing to a peak,
as the sun, rising, radiates goodness and life
into the silent room - and into my heart.

Daylight temporarily filling the empty space.
A weaker proxy for the Unconditional Love
Sun shined into the world, my world.

Sun would have Loved this day.
Embracing the Light and this present moment,
always choosing to focus on Happiness and Love.

So, I will choose to Love this day, too.
I will find peaceful ways to Love this day,
for her.

Love *Be*

Causes

You are limitless.

The causes you create
with your Light
expand boundlessly
in time and space.

Ripples of your thoughts,
words and actions
flow to infinity.

Merging with and increasing
waves of probabilities and potentials.
Or, causing waves to flow
in another direction.

A great responsibility,
yet a beautiful, easy joy,
for each of us to embrace

when the protection of
Unconditional Love
for all living beings
guides our inspirations.

Interlude: **Skylark Moment**

Walking along a path bejewelled with opened flint pebbles, partially embedded in the dry mud and clay.

Grasses glint and ripple in the sun, tender green blades reflecting countless micro rainbows along the edges of tiny refracting surfaces.

The trees swaying to the song of a blackbird and the sweet high calls of feathered parents and their chicks, foraging in the branches.

Over the nearby meadow, a fluting meme of delight emanates gently from the sky as a rare Skylark floats invisibly high above, gracing the ground with rolling, tinkling song.

How many others in the past have known such blissful moments? How many chances remain in the future?

May we tenderly care for these places, beings and moments with Love and protect them. Then, give them back to the Universe and to the future of those who may also be blessed to know them.

Love *Be*

Kaleidoscope Dreams

Conscious in deep sleep dreams,
awakening to the mind's
raw process of creation.

The building blocks revealing themselves.
Incredible living mosaics and
intricate kaleidoscopic arrays.

Mesmerizing moving patterns.
glimpsed within the sleeping dream factory
that we normally do not see.

The machinery of perceived reality,
silently working,
creating.

We awake and climb from our beds,
walk onto our kaleidoscopic stage and believe this
perception is different to a dream.

Love *Be*

Record Player

Inner recordings,
stuck on repeat,
replaying and relaying
past perceptions.

Creating obstructions to
experiencing now,
Love and Happiness
in this present moment.

Notice.
Let it go.
Choose the gift of Love.
In this case, for oneself.

Love *Be*

Peace-fuel

Peacefuelled insight flows
when inner interruption goes.

What we choose to consume
into our mind,

think and talk about,

is as important
as food and water,

creating the causes
for thoughts and actions.

Peacefuel
energises
Love.

Love *Be*

Shape-shifting

Our forms may change
but we do not end
because we were never entirely
in one place
in the first place.

Love *Be*

The Wind

We listen to her choir, in darkness.
The wind visits tonight,
unleashing her energy with abandon,
in all the forms of motion she can muster.

Tonight is her time to be
all that she can be. Owning the sky,
her excited atoms race in waves. Flowing
air rivers, challenging anything "solid".

Her concert is to be heard in all its breadth.
She plays a symphony of the deepest rumbles,
the highest discernible whistles, and
the white noise of countless leaves in motion.

Tomorrow, will reveal again her loving aspect.
She will gift soft flight to baby spiders,
invisibly lifting the delicate scent of flowers
and carrying a child's laughter in her soft hands.

The Steadied Particle

In a thought,
in a perception,
in an instant,
a particle steadies
and we believe
it is real.

And, for us,
it temporarily,
is.
Within created perception
made of senses
that are formed of

steadied particles
of vibrating,
no thing –
except the potential
to be
Everything.

Which makes life,
even more precious.
Within a moment,
touch a flower
with this knowledge
and see living Love.

Bird song, Soul Song

My soul floats,
in bird song.
Exquisite, joyful, vibrant
colours of sweet, pure beauty.

Pure notes of life energy,
Light shining from Nature's breath.
Songs beyond measure that fill the woods,
grace the meadows and the skies.

Music gifted to the air,
joining with the gentle sounds
of Nature, and the vibration of this
temporary, magical appearance.

The music of pure essence,
woven through my mind and soul since birth,
bringing Life, Joy, Peace, nourishment and happiness,
as do you, my dear family and friends.

Now, with the breathing trees,
the silent whisper of clouds,
gently moving. Peaceful,
within the pure Light.

Bird song appears in countless notes,
ending and not ending,
everywhere and no where.
In Love and Peace.

Love *Be*

Light Presence

Remember.
The Light
is always there.

Always present,
behind, within
and through,

everything.

Chapter 2

Wishes

Love *Be*

A wish for the journey of you

At the beginning of the story.

In the middle of the story.

and at the end of the story.

may your heart be

Happy.

Love *Be*

A wish for your spring-times

May you and all living beings experience gentle green Springtimes of hope, joy, love, comfort, abundance and peace after life's harsh Winters.

Perpetual Springtimes so lovely that all difficulty is washed away, as if it had never existed.

Springtimes so exquisitely fresh that joyful healing and peace fills all corners of the world, and all corners of all minds and hearts.

Love *Be*

A wish for your present moment

May your living
present moment
be joy-filled with
peaceful consciousness,
and feel as expansive as
the Universe
and as deep as
the limitless ocean of
Unconditional Love.

This is IT.
Right now.
Happy New Moment!
All increments are illusory.
Happy New Second.
Happy New Minute.
Happy New Hour.
Happy New Day.
Happy New Year.

Happy.
Now.

Love *Be*

A wish for your wellness

May you always be blessed to
feel the musical notes of wellness
singing in your soul and form.

Essential wellness singing within peaceful
clarity when the noise of thought
settles gently to allow you to, simply be.

Wellness, within the limitless calm
continuum of awake silence
that vibrates in notes of colours.

Wellness singing with the potential
of all good energy that is present now.
and, will be.

A wish for your community

May you always be
surrounded
by those who
accept you warmly,
cherish your unique gifts
and give you the tender
companionship,
freedom
and support

to flourish.

A wish for your beautiful light

May your inner and outer world
be filled with Joy, Love, Peace,
Wellbeing and Light.

Where the Light seems hidden
may you quickly find it,
or, create it.

If others cannot find their Light,
may you find it for them,
within yourself.

May every being you encounter
be filled with the joy of Love and Kindness
they experience through You.

Love *Be*

Meditation

I open my heart to Peace.

Breathing slowly.

I breathe in light and blessings.

I breathe out Love.

Love *Be*

Kind words for a troubled world

While praying for peace, these words appeared to mind.

"When the world around appears to be in disarray and it appears we and others might be in harms way, with no tangible option to control or prevent events, take refuge in the loving kindness within your own heart and pray.

Show Kindness and give Unconditional Love in any way you can to all living beings; to a spider, to mammals, to all residents of a tree or forest, to people, to beings living on a blade of grass, to a bird, to the beauty of the sky.

Whether in thought or deed, big or small, acts of loving kindness from your heart will help to counteract the harmful disease of anger in the world, now and in the future. Creating beneficial ripples that will extend far beyond the edges of the idea of self and now.

There are a million (at least) opportunities for micro kindnesses to choose from in every moment and every single one makes a difference. This we can control."

Love *Be*

About this book

The writings and illustrations in this book are personal creative expressions born from meditative experiences, spiritual study and time immersed in Nature.

The poem *'The Only Thing"* was inspired many years ago by a near death experience. There was a profound transformative perception of a force of Light, Love and Peace that was far beyond ordinary experiences.

It was such a powerful experience, I was initially unable to talk about it for a very long time. I felt the message perceived during this experience was important and wished to share it, here, in the poem, *The Only Thing*.

The pen and ink drawings in this book are left empty of colour as a visual expression of how our inner narrative and what we choose to consume and hold in our mind can colour what we perceive. Unconditional Love has the power to change perceptions and illuminate our world in beautiful ways.

Love *Be*

Thank you

To Family and Friends near and far, past and present, thank you for supporting my creative endeavours with Love and kind encouragement thoughout life.

To Mum, thank you for lovingly supporting my childhood passions for reading, writing and art, and for enthusiastically encouraging me to publish my poems. I am so grateful for the Love, care and kindness that you have selflessly given and for everything you have done for us. Love You.

To Dad, thank you for your steady, loving faith in my strengths, helping to keep me focused on bringing this book to fruition, and for your Love, kindness, care and encouragements. Love You.

To Spiritual Teachers, throughout time and present now, thank you for sharing your wisdom and transformative kindness with me and with all those who are ready to listen.

To Christopher John Payne, thank you for your generous expert publishing guidance, professional insights and kind, focused encouragement.

To the beauty of Nature, thank you for the lifelong inspiration.

Dedication

This book is dedicated to the flourishing of Love, Kindness, Wellbeing, Peace and Happiness for all living beings.

May all living beings have beautiful, happy, healthy and safe homes, peaceful nature-filled environments and all the resources they need to feel contented and joyful.

Printed in Dunstable, United Kingdom